The Wild World of Animals

Tigers

Striped Stalkers

by Adele D. Richardson

Consultant:
Tammy Quist
President
The Wildcat Society

Bridgestone Books
an imprint of Capstone Press
Mankato, Minnesota

Bridgestone Books are published by Capstone Press
151 Good Counsel Drive, P.O. Box 669, Mankato, Minnesota 56002
http://www.capstone-press.com

Library of Congress Cataloging-in-Publication Data
Richardson, Adele, 1966–
   Tigers : striped stalkers / by Adele D. Richardson.
   p. cm.—(The wild world of animals)
   Includes bibliographical references (p. 24) and index.
   Summary: A brief introduction to tigers, describing their physical characteristics,
habitat, young, food, predators, and relationship to people.
   ISBN 0-7368-1140-0
   1. Tigers—Juvenile literature. [1. Tigers.] I. Title. II. Series.
QL737.C23 R526 2002
599.756—dc21   2001003946

Editorial Credits
Megan Schoeneberger, editor; Karen Risch, product planning editor; Linda Clavel,
   designer and illustrator; Heidi Schoof, photo researcher

Photo Credits
Amrit P. Singh/GeoIMAGERY, 10
Corel, 6
International Stock/Mark Newman, cover; Michael Agliolo, 12
Kenneth W. Fink/Root Resources, 4
Mark Newman/TOM STACK & ASSOCIATES, 20
Michael Turco, 14
PhotoDisc, Inc., 1, 16, (texture) cover, 2, 3, 6, 8, 10, 16, 22, 23, 24
Visuals Unlimited/Inga Spence, 8
Wendy Kaveney, 18

1 2 3 4 5 6 07 06 05 04 03 02

Table of Contents

tail

teeth

claws

Tigers

Tigers are large, wild cats. They have four legs, a long tail, and sharp claws and teeth. Most tigers have orange fur with dark brown or black stripes. Adult tigers are about 9 feet (3 meters) long. Male tigers are larger than female tigers.

FUN FACTS

No two tigers have the same pattern of stripes.

Tigers Are Mammals

Tigers are mammals. Mammals are warm-blooded and have a backbone. Female mammals give birth to live young. A young mammal drinks milk from its mother. Most mammals have fur to keep warm.

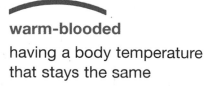

warm-blooded
having a body temperature that stays the same

FUN FACTS

Tigers are the largest members of the cat family. They are larger than lions.

A Tiger's Habitat

All wild tigers live in Asia. Siberian tigers live in cold, snowy forests. Chinese and Indo-Chinese tigers live on mountains. Bengal and Sumatran tigers live in the rain forest. Tigers need habitats with plenty of space, food, and water.

habitat
the place where an animal lives

FUN FACTS ! Tigers can run as fast as 30 miles (48 kilometers) per hour.

Stalking Prey

Tigers are carnivores. They eat only meat. They hunt buffalo and deer for food. Tigers sometimes eat monkeys. Tigers usually stalk at night. They hide when they see prey. A tiger trips its prey from behind. The tiger then bites the prey's neck with its sharp teeth.

stalk

to hunt an animal in a quiet, secret way

Mating and Birth

Most adult tigers live alone. Male and female tigers come together to mate. The male tiger leaves after mating. The female gives birth to a litter about 15 weeks later. Two or three young tigers are born in a litter.

litter
a group of animals born at the same time to the same mother

Tiger Cubs

Young tigers are called cubs. Cubs weigh 2 to 3 pounds (1 to 1.4 kilograms) at birth. Cubs are blind for two weeks. A cub drinks milk from its mother for eight weeks. The mother then teaches the cub how to hunt. Cubs stay with their mothers for about two years.

A tiger's roar can be heard up to 2 miles (3.2 kilometers) away.

Predators

Tigers have few predators. Hyenas or other tigers sometimes attack tiger cubs. A tiger mother protects her cubs. She shows her teeth and growls to scare away predators. The mother attacks if a predator will not leave. She then moves her cubs to a safer place.

predator
an animal that hunts and eats other animals

Tiger Territories

Tigers have their own territories in a habitat. Tigers mark their territory with scents. They claw tree trunks. Tigers sometimes scratch the ground with their claws. These scents and claw marks warn other tigers and animals to stay away.

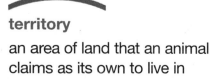

territory

an area of land that an animal claims as its own to live in

Tigers and People

People help tigers by putting them in reserves. Reserves are protected areas of land for animals. Some countries have laws against hunting tigers. Tigers help people in nearby villages. They kill the deer and monkeys that destroy the villagers' crops.

Hands On: Tiger Size

Tigers are the biggest cats in the world. Many tigers are about 9 feet (3 meters) long. This activity will let you see how your size compares to a tiger's size.

What You Need

Two pencils
A yardstick or meter stick

What You Do

1. Lie down on the floor with your feet against a wall or closed door. Lay one pencil on the floor just above your head. Leave the pencil on the floor.
2. Lay the yardstick or meter stick on the floor so you measure 1 yard (1 meter) away from the wall or door.
3. Put your finger at the end of the stick. Now place the stick on the other side of your finger so you measure another yard or meter. Do this one more time and you will measure 9 feet (3 meters).
4. Place the other pencil on the floor at the end of the stick.

Measure from pencil to pencil and you can see how much longer a tiger is than you. Is anything in your home as large as a tiger?

Words to Know

carnivore (KAR-nuh-vor)—an animal that eats only meat

mammal (MAM-uhl)—a warm-blooded animal that has a backbone and feeds milk to its young

mate (MATE)—to join together to produce young; male and female tigers mate to produce tiger cubs.

predator (PRED-uh-tur)—an animal that hunts and eats other animals

prey (PRAY)—an animal that is hunted by another animal for food

reserve (ree-ZURV)—a protected area where animals can have space to live and food to eat

territory (TER-uh-tor-ee)—an area of land that an animal claims as its own to live in

Read More

Claybourne, Anna. *Tiger.* Killer Creatures. Austin, Texas: Raintree Steck-Vaughn, 2001.

Schafer, Susan. *Tigers.* Animals, Animals. New York: Marshall Cavendish, 2000.

Welsbacher, Anne. *Tigers.* Wild Cats. Edina, Minn.: Abdo, 2000.

Internet Sites

Cyber Tiger @ nationalgeographic.com
http://www.nationalgeographic.com/features/97/tigers/maina.html

The Wildcat Society—Tiger
http://www.wildcatsociety.org/catalog/big%20cats/tiger.html

Index